LEADERSHIP ETHICS

LEADERSHIP ETHICS

Is Doing the Right Thing Enough?

LAMAR ODOM, J.D.

Copyright © 2010 by Lamar Odom.

Library of Congress Control Number: 2010908115
ISBN: Hardcover   978-1-4535-1400-9
              Softcover   978-1-4535-1399-6
              Ebook   978-1-4535-1401-6

All rights reserved. No part of this book may be reproduced or transmitted in any form or by any means, electronic or mechanical, including photocopying, recording, or by any information storage and retrieval system, without permission in writing from the copyright owner.

This book was printed in the United States of America.

To order additional copies of this book, contact:
Xlibris Corporation
1-888-795-4274
www.Xlibris.com
Orders@Xlibris.com
81778

CONTENTS

Acknowledgments 9
Introduction 11

Chapter 1: What Is Ethics? 17
Chapter 2: Understanding Common Ethical Paradigms 27
Chapter 3: Why Leaders Fail to Act Ethically 39
Chapter 4: The Problem with Doing the Right Thing 53
Chapter 5: Is Ethical Reasoning and Ethics
             Training Important? 61
Chapter 6: Ethicality of Transactional versus
             Transformational Leadership 73
Chapter 7: Strategies for Resolving Ethical Dilemmas 87
Chapter 8: Conclusion 97

To my children. My loving daughter, Alexis J. Odom—you are my inspiration and the reason I do what I do. My sons, whom I am most proud of, Julius and Marques Odom—I hope you will learn from my mistakes and emulate my successes. It is my desire that each of you may find this book useful as you grow and tackle the challenges that you will inevitably face in this journey called life. Hopefully, when you face your ethical dilemmas, in some small way, you may find somewhere embedded in these pages the insight and inspiration you need to make the right decision.

ACKNOWLEDGMENTS

THIS BOOK COULD not have been completed without the encouragement, support, and loving patience of my lifelong friend Mary Brown. Thank you, Mary, for contributing your knowledge as an educator to making this journey a success.

INTRODUCTION

AS A LEADERSHIP professor and ethics consultant, I have conducted corporate training and taught hundreds of courses on this intriguing topic. When I ask, "What is ethics?" the response I most often receive is "Ethics is doing the right thing." Whether I address the question to students or corporate executives, I most often receive that cliché response more than any other. Over time, I became increasingly troubled by this seemingly universal response to the question. Was ethics that simple as just "doing the right thing"? I concluded that it was not. While, ultimately, ethics is *about* doing the right thing, defining ethics in such a manner minimizes the complexity of the various types of ethical dilemmas leaders face. Although the desired end result is to *do the right thing,* when confronted with ethical challenges, leaders often have difficulty achieving this simple goal. Moreover, sometimes the right thing may, on the surface, appear to be the wrong thing. For example, some folks may argue that telling the truth is always the right thing to do. However, is it wrong to misrepresent the truth if doing so would prevent others from being harmed? If a robber entered a home and asked the father if he knew the combination to the panic room where his children were hiding, should the father tell the truth? Is torture the right thing to do if it will gain information that could save innocent lives? What if the combatant being tortured is a child? These are just a few examples of how complex ethical challenges may not be easily resolved by applying the principle of just do the right thing. While doing the right thing is important, the process of achieving the right result is equally important. Leaders must ensure that they avoid using an unethical process to achieve an ethical result. In other words, the end should not always justify the means even if the end result is ultimately the right thing. The process and the result must both be ethical.

When leaders fail to act ethically, those with whom they are entrusted to lead inevitably lose confidence in the leaders' ability to carry out the mission. When followers lose trust in their leader, his or her effectiveness is diminished and the leader may find that he or she is in the midst of a leadership crisis. That is the precise sentiment of many Americans regarding our nation's leaders. According to a U.S. news and a Harvard University poll, many Americans believe we are experiencing a leadership crisis. The evidence of this crisis transcends all professions and disciplines. It touches all organizations including corporate America, nonprofits, government, academia, and even our most sacred religious institutions. In the current media, it is not uncommon to read stories about personal ethical failures. Whether the focus is from political leaders like Governors Mark Sanford and Eliot Spitzer, or sports figures and corporate pitchmen like Tiger Woods, behaving ethically is a challenge that all leaders face. When viewed closely, one can readily conclude that there is an ethical dimension to every decision a leader makes, or as Joanne B. Ciulla, a leading ethics scholar, so accurately states, "Ethics is the heart of leadership."

Now, although ethics may be at the heart of leadership, I believe power is the sine qua non of leadership ethics. I believe this to be true because power is the essential ingredient that enables leaders to influence followers toward a common goal. Without the ability to influence others to follow, the leader lacks the ability to lead. The leader's power is the fuel that propels his leadership effectiveness. According to the seminal research of two prominent social scientists, French and Raven, leaders possess various types of power. They may have *expert power* based on their level of knowledge or expertise in a certain field. Leaders may possess *referent power* due to their innate personality, charisma, and ability to inspire. Every leader, due to her being in a position of authority, has *reward* and *coercive* power. So it is the leader's power that serves as the catalyst for influence and is ultimately what makes the leader effective.

Is effectiveness the test of leadership? Should we judge leaders solely by their ability to get things done? Osama bin Laden and Hitler, by most accounts, would be considered "effective" leaders. They were able to influence and mobilize their followers toward a specific goal. Both achieved the desired results, and the former was able to inspire his followers to make the ultimate sacrifice. In both examples, their effectiveness was directly related to their use of power—referent, reward, and in some cases, coercive. However, most people would not consider bin Laden or Hitler to be ethical leaders—effective leaders, yes; good leaders, no. When a leader uses his or her power ethically to do good—*and* good is assessed based upon reason and objectivity, not the subjective intentions of the leader—the leader is most often perceived to have acted ethically. Thus, ethical leadership is synonymous with good leadership, good as defined by reason and objectivity, not as defined subjectively in the minds of the leader or his followers. Thus, while the actions of a terrorist and his followers in killing innocent people may be perceived as good in the eyes of the terrorist, when evaluated using reason and objectivity, the behavior of killing innocent people would not be considered good. Therefore, when leaders fail to behave ethically, their failure is most often the result of their unethical use of power. When a leader uses power properly, ethical results, good results are most often achieved; by the same token, the misuse of power often results in unethical behavior and, ultimately, bad results.

This book is designed to give the nascent and established leader a basic understanding of the challenges of leadership ethics while offering some practical strategies to help facilitate resolving ethical dilemmas. It is not intended to serve as a comprehensive evaluation of ethical theories or principles. Although some will be addressed, the primary purpose is to provide the reader with a simple and concise background to a subject that is paradoxically simple yet complex.

CHAPTER 1

What Is Ethics?

WHEN ASKED, "WHAT is ethics?" most people have a basic idea. Ethics is a discipline we all know *something* about. Simply stated, ethics is about trying to engage in right versus wrong behavior. However, while this may be true, ethical dilemmas that leaders face are often more complex and often cannot be resolved with simple ethical reasoning. In other words, simply doing what may be perceived as *the right thing* does not necessarily provide the guidance to resolve complex ethical situations. With that notion in mind, I challenge you to think of ethics from a more critical perspective. Therefore, I offer the following definition of *ethics*. Ethics is a philosophical discipline that focuses on right and wrong. By defining ethics as a discipline of philosophy, I am simply stating that ethics connotes a way of thinking or reasoning. However, while ethics involves discerning right and wrong behavior, it is also about so much more. It is about how we get to the right behavior. More importantly, ethics is about what we *ought* to do when faced with ethical dilemmas evaluated from a perspective of reason and objectivity. The latter part of that statement is very important because by using reason and objectivity, the leader avoids the mistake of deciding behavior based solely on what she personally believes, relying more on an objective analysis of the facts while making reasonable assumptions and inferences, and finally, drawing reasonable conclusions versus making a decision because she believes within her gut that such decision is the right course of action.

Now, incorporating a reasoned and objective analysis is where a clear distinction can be drawn between ethics and morality. Although the terms are often used interchangeably, *morality* tends to be more subjective. For example, stoning a woman for adultery may be considered moral by an individual whose religion espouses such views. However, with an ethical analysis of such behavior based on reason and objectivity, this could not rationally be justified. First of all, a reasoned and objective argument would have to consider an analysis of the punishment in relation to the wrong behavior. A reasoned argument must match an appropriate level of punishment with the crime. Thus, to take life when life has not been taken would seem to violate that principle. Therefore, ethical behavior is based on a broader societal view. So in the eyes of the leader who wishes to stone the adulterer because he subjectively believes it is the right thing to do, his behavior would be moral. However, as just illustrated, applying an ethical analysis based on reason and objectivity would lead to a different conclusion. This may lead one to ponder the question, is ethics and morality related? Of course, but as just illustrated, they can also be differentiated.

Now that I've defined ethics and drawn a distinction between ethics and morality, let's explore some of the underlying tenets of ethical behavior. In my review of hundreds of articles written about the discipline of ethics, a common theme consistently emerges. I believe that theme expresses a fundamental tenet of ethics, and that is, ethics is centered on the objective of showing concern for the well-being of others. Another way of phrasing it is ethics is about avoiding doing harm to others. Think about it; one of the primary tenets of the Hippocratic oath, which provides guidance to the behavior of the physician community, is to "first do no harm." One of the most egregious examples of the violation of this principle was the Tuskegee syphilis study, which was conducted by the U.S. Department of Public Health physicians and scientists in the 1930s. In this study, hundreds of poor African American men were used as guinea pigs by the government to study the effects of syphilis. The men were deceived into believing that they were being treated for "bad blood" when, in fact, they were experimental subjects. Even upon the discovery of penicillin, these men were still denied care, and the experiment continued for over forty years. If the leaders involved in the Tuskegee study had followed the ethical principle of showing concern for the interest of others, the outcome and treatment of these men would have been different. Had the physicians and scientists sought to do no harm, when penicillin became the treatment protocol for syphilis, care would not have been withheld. The ethical principle of showing concern for the interest others must guide all ethical-decision making.

If ethical behavior is predicated on showing concern for the interest of others, what precludes leaders from following that principle? What precludes leaders from engaging in ethical decisions that do not harm others? This question will be addressed in greater detail in the next chapter, but the answer can be found in one word—*egocentrism*. When leaders pursue their own self-interest even when doing so will knowingly cause harm to others, the outcome will often result in unethical behavior. Upon a review of the many examples cited in the introduction of this book, one will readily see the prevalence of egocentric thinking guiding the behavior of the various leaders. If ethics is at the heart of leadership, egocentrism is at the heart of all unethical behavior.

In chapter 3, I address in greater detail the reasons why leaders fail to act ethically, but before moving on, I want to address one other perspective of ethics that is often manifested when I engage in corporate training. Many people often confuse ethical behavior with religion, law, or societal mores. The research of Dr. Linda Elder and Dr. Richard Paul clearly point out the conflict that often exists between these various disciplines. Although I will provide a few examples here, for a more in-depth analysis of the relationship between these two disciplines, I encourage you to read some of the writings of Dr. Elder and Dr. Paul. You can find their work by visiting the Foundation for Critical Thinking at www.criticalthinking.org.

It is not uncommon in my healthcare law and ethics course for students to equate legal behavior with ethical behavior. Although there are common goals (e.g., they both seek the common good, and both address issues of right and wrong behavior), there are fundamental differences between the two. The following example illustrates this point.

Dr. Smith is driving home and comes upon an accident. Dr. Smith is a trained emergency physician, whose services clearly could make a difference to the injured parties. Unfortunately for the victims, Dr. Smith refuses to stop and render assistance. Did Dr. Smith have a legal duty to stop and render aid? Did he have an ethical duty to stop and render aid?

When I use this hypothetical in class, most students respond that he had both. However, unless Dr. Smith had a contractual relationship with the injured parties, he had no legal duty. American jurisprudence does not impose a general duty among physicians to render aid. At this point, a student will often raise the Good Samaritan argument. Although most states have a Good Samaritan statute, this law does not impose a legal duty to act. In fact, the objective of the law is to encourage physicians and regular citizens to do something they are not otherwise required to do. The law attempts to encourage physicians who are not required to render assistance to do so. In other words, the law encourages them to be a Good Samaritan. Such laws afford protection from civil lawsuit if they act as Good Samaritans and are subsequently sued for negligent behavior. In other words, this statute attempts to encourage doctors to be Good Samaritans because in those situations, they have no legal duty to act. Now, many would argue, and I would agree, that there is an ethical duty to stop and render assistance. Doing so would be consistent with one of the previously discussed principles of ethical behavior—showing concern for the interest of others. It is worth noting here that laws tell us what we *must* do; ethics addresses what we *ought* to do. Moreover, what is legal may not always be ethical, and what is ethical is not always required by the law.

As just illustrated, sometimes legal behavior and ethical behavior may conflict and yield different results. Another example of this conflict is seen in how the law, particularly federal law, fails to protect sexual orientation. Many argue for the repeal of the military's "don't ask, don't tell" policy on ethical grounds. While the law does not provide sexual orientation protection to gay men and women openly serving in the military, many view discrimination against this group to be unethical.

While ethics can be distinguished from law, similar arguments can be made regarding the nexus between religion, social mores, and ethical behavior. For many years, laws and social mores prevented interracial marriage. In fact, it was not until the U.S. Supreme Court decided on *Loving v. Virginia* in 1967 that laws preventing interracial marriage were declared unconstitutional. Today, as a result of religious views and social mores regarding this topic, same-sex marriage is viewed the same way. Although one may make a cogent argument on religious grounds, is it ethical to deny two people the right to exercise their liberty interest in the form of marriage? If a primary tenet of ethics is showing concern for others and seeking to avoid harming others, can this policy be considered ethical? Unfortunately, religious behavior and ethical behavior are often viewed synonymously; however, while the disciplines are similar, ethical reasoning must go beyond that required for religion. If one uses religious reasoning solely as the basis for resolving ethical dilemmas, conflict will inevitably occur. For example, which religious perspective should be followed? Let's take a look at another example to illustrate this potential conflict.

A mother brings her infant child to the emergency room. The emergency room physicians determine that a blood transfusion is necessary to save the life of the child. The mother is a Jehovah's Witness, and her faith prohibits blood transfusions. From a religious perspective, allowing the child to die would be the required course of action notwithstanding that a blood transfusion would save her life. However, through ethical reasoning and the principles of showing concern for the interest of others and evaluating the situation based on reason and objectivity, it is more likely that one would conclude that granting the blood transfusion would be the proper course of action. Of course, the law is well settled in this area, making it legal to give the transfusion even if it were against the mother's wishes. The point here is not to suggest that law, religion, or social mores do not or should not play a part in ethical decision-making; of course, they do. In fact, considering the law or religious tenets may be a great starting point. However, they should be just that, starting points. Ethical analysis must go beyond the law or what one's religion may require. Ethical analysis must address the concern of minimizing harm to others and avoiding egocentrism, and such analysis must be done based on reason and objectivity.

In this chapter, a working definition of ethics has been developed. In addition, I've compared and contrasted ethics with other disciplines such as law and religion. Through several examples, I've illustrated how ethical analysis and reasoning, while inclusive of law and religion, must sometimes go beyond the requirements of law and religion in an attempt to reach an ethical outcome. Finally, the notion of egocentrism was introduced as a common roadblock to ethical behavior. The next chapter will address some common ethical paradigms that impact how leaders resolve ethical dilemmas.

CHAPTER 2

Understanding Common Ethical Paradigms

ETHICS IS THE philosophical discipline that explores right and wrong behavior within the context of what one ought to do. Ethics is concerned with the ideal behavior—what one should do versus the common norms or behavior that one engages in. During recent years, ethics, and particularly ethics in business, has received more attention due primarily to the many corporate scandals that occurred during the turn of the century. As a result, organizations have placed more emphasis on ethics training. In most business schools, students are required to take at least one ethics course, where they are introduced to various ethical theories. This chapter will provide a brief overview of some common ethical paradigms that every leader should be familiar with.

One of the most common ethical theories is utilitarianism. This is one of the most popular theories applied to resolving ethical dilemmas, in part, because it is a simple theory to grasp and apply. The utilitarian theory suggests that when faced with an ethical dilemma, one should pursue the course of action that brings about the greater good for the benefit of the majority. Many actions can be justified from a utilitarian perspective. The Fifth Amendment to the U.S. Constitution allows for the state to take private property as long as it serves a public use and just compensation is paid for that property. This is known as eminent domain and is based on the principle of utilitarian ethics. The founding fathers knew that there would be times when the individual would be expected to sacrifice for the greater good—the larger community. The right to own private property is an important part of American culture. It was so important that the founding fathers deemed it necessary to include it as an express right in the Constitution by declaring that "no person shall be denied life, liberty, or property without due process." However, this important right can be denied for the purpose of achieving the greater good for the majority. Therefore, seizing private land under eminent domain to build a road or a hospital can be justified under the ethical principle of utilitarianism.

Another example of utilitarianism can be observed in decisions to go to war or decisions that are often made in the act of war. Was it ethical to drop the atomic bomb during World War II? Before answering that question, it is important to again address the subtle difference between ethics and morality. While both are concerned with issues of right and wrong behavior, morality is most often viewed in the eyes of the individual. Therefore, a person may believe that misogyny is acceptable and fits within his moral perspective of women. Or a person may be a racist and find such beliefs to be morally acceptable. Therefore, when employment decisions need to be made in the workplace, this person may find nothing wrong with denying women or minorities equal opportunities. He may find nothing morally wrong with discriminating against such groups. Morals are personal values that individuals use to guide their behavior. A person's morals may be influenced by a variety of factors: family, church, society, religion, education, media, etc. The important distinction is that one's moral behavior is personal and, thus, subjective. In other words, morality is in the eyes of the beholder.

Ethics, as has been previously defined, is based on objectivity. Therefore, ethics requires one to look at women or minorities and evaluate them, taking into consideration factors outside their race or gender. Moreover, ethics seeks to establish a standard of behavior that governs members of a group. This is necessary because everyone may have different moral views; therefore, their behavior may be inconsistent with others. Ethics seeks to bring some standardization to that behavior. The U.S. Military has an ethical code that prohibits discrimination based on race or gender. Therefore, while the racist may personally feel his behavior is acceptable, such actions would be inconsistent with the military's code of ethical conduct.

So getting back to the question of the ethicality of dropping the atomic bomb, applying utilitarian principles, one may conclude that it was the right thing to do. This is the ethical dilemma President Truman faced leading up to that dreadful decision that he was forced to make. According to historical reports, when the *atomic bomb* was dropped on *Hiroshima*, the plane crew was silent. Captain Lewis allegedly uttered six words, "My god, what have we done?" Three days later, another one fell on *Nagasaki*. About 152,000 were killed; many times, more were wounded and burned to die later. The next day, Japan sued for peace. When deciding whether to use "the most terrible weapon ever known," President Truman appointed an *interim committee* made up of distinguished and responsible people in the *government*. Most, but not all, of its military advisors supported using the atomic bomb. Top-level *scientists* said they could find no acceptable alternative to using it, but they were opposed by equally able *scientists*. After lengthy discussions, the committee decided that the lives saved by ending the war swiftly by using this weapon outweighed the lives destroyed by using it and thought that the best course of action. This line of reasoning is consistent with a utilitarian analysis. The decision was made pursuing the course of action that brought about the greater good for the majority. Was it the right decision? Was the utilitarian approach the proper course of action?

Utilitarian ethics is not without critics. Many would argue that one major problem with this approach to solving ethical dilemmas is that it overlooks the rights of the minority. What about the person whose land is being seized? Is it fair to that person? What about the 150,000 who were killed in dropping the atomic bomb? Was it fair to them to sacrifice their lives for the greater good? Is serving the greater good always the right course of action to take? For those who do not subscribe to this ethical principle, there is another ethical theory that is more absolute; that is the theory of deontology.

The ethical theory of deontology advances the notion that our actions should be guided by a moral duty or imperative. When faced with an ethical dilemma, this overarching imperative should guide one's decision. A simple application of deontological ethics can be illustrated with the question of whether it is ethical to torture. The deontologist would argue that torture is inhuman because it causes physical or emotional harm to the individual. Humans have a moral imperative not to torture one another. The deontologist would hold firm to this imperative even if doing so would result in obtaining information that would save the lives of others.

Another example of deontology may be observed in the recent healthcare debate. One of the chief provisions of the health reform act is the expansion of coverage to those who currently do not have access to healthcare. For many years, healthcare scholars have debated the question of whether healthcare is a right or privilege. A deontologist would make the argument that life is sacred and access to a basic level of healthcare is a moral imperative. In other words, healthcare is a right, and denial of such would be unethical. As you can see by now, the deontological approach is very black-and-white. There are no gray areas. All ethical dilemmas are resolved by following whatever moral imperative governs the situation. In many respects, it would seem that applying the ethical principle of deontology would make ethical decisions easy for a leader. However, the deontological approach is not without its critics. Can ethical dilemmas always be reduced to application of a simple moral imperative? To illustrate this point, let's revisit the moral duty to always tell the truth. Is it ever ethical to lie? The Bible commands, "Thou shalt not lie." Therefore, when faced with a dilemma of lying or telling the truth, the decision is simple—tell the truth. Well, let's think about this dilemma a little closer. What about the burglar situation previously mentioned? Would it be unethical to lie to the burglar? In a situation when lying prevents others from being harmed, is it not the right thing to do? Of course, the deontologist would answer this question in the negative. However, when considering the ethical principles of avoiding harming others and showing concern for the interest of others, it would appear that in some situations, lying may be justified. Therefore, if a leader relies solely on the ethical principle of deontology, he may find that such an absolutist approach may lead to its own set of challenges when faced with certain types of ethical dilemmas.

The next ethical principle was introduced in chapter 1. It is probably the least accepted by modern-day ethicists, and it has the potential to be the most harmful in impeding ethical behavior. The ethical theory of egoism advances the principle that one has a moral duty to engage in behavior that advances his own self-interest. Moreover, advancing one's own self-interest may be pursued even at the expense of others. This is the aspect of egocentrism that many ethicists find quite troubling. The impact of this course of action and its obvious potential to impede ethical behavior was addressed in chapter 1, so there is no need to revisit it here other than to reiterate the notion that egocentrism is one of the primary reasons leaders fail to act ethically.

The final ethical principle that merits some discussion is that of justice. The principle of justice dates back over two thousand years ago to Aristotle, who espoused the notion of treating others equally. In addition to equality, justice also connotes fairness. It would be hard to consider whether behavior is ethical without taking into consideration the issues of fairness and equality. The founding fathers understood the importance of this principle by embedding it in the Constitution. The Fifth Amendment allows the government to take property from a private individual provided that such property is taken for public use and the individual receives *just* compensation. This is known as the takings clause, and two ethical principles seem to justify such action. First, such property is being taken for the greater good, which is a utilitarian principle, and the second requirement of just compensation advances the principle of justice by ensuring equality and fairness.

What does it mean to be fair? The term *fairness* is an elusive concept. Fairness has two core components: outcome fairness or what social scientists call distributive justice and the psychology of the fair process or what social scientists refer to as procedural justice. Procedural justice typically means that one must be afforded some level of due process. In other words, a person is due a process that provides them with notice and opportunity for a hearing. The requirement of procedural justice builds trust and commitment. In turn, trust and commitment produce voluntary cooperation and belief in the process or action that is being taken by the institution. Ethical behavior demands that if a person is being denied an entitlement or some type of basic right, they should be afforded procedural due process before that right is taken away.

Although procedural justice ensures that a person receives notice and a hearing, distributive justice seeks to ensure that the decision or action taken leads to a fair outcome. Therefore, distributive justice seeks to distribute or allocate benefits and burdens equitably. The psychology of outcome fairness or distributive justice is also illustrated in the Fifth Amendment's takings clause. Although private property may be taken, doing so may be reconciled with ethical behavior if the person whose property is condemned receives just compensation. When people receive the compensation, resources, or reward that they believe they deserve, they feel satisfied with the outcome. Moreover, when people are satisfied with the outcome, they will reciprocate by accepting the action as being a fair resolution to the dilemma. Note that the ethical principle of justice, whether procedural or distributive, focuses on the consequences or outcome of one's behavior. Therefore, this ethical principle is teleological/utilitarian in nature. Unlike deontology, which is duty driven, teleological ethics focuses on the results or consequences of one's actions.

The various ethical paradigms and principles discussed in this chapter help shape how we resolve ethical dilemmas. In some instances, the decision will be the same regardless of the ethical theory applied. However, in other instances, the outcome may differ, depending upon which theory is used. When faced with an ethical dilemma, a leader may decide to use a utilitarian approach, or he may decide to make a decision based solely on a moral imperative. Regardless of the approach used, egocentrism may have an impact on whether the leader makes an ethical or unethical decision. Therefore, the next chapter will probe further into the relationship between egocentrism and leadership behavior by exploring some of the reasons *why leaders fail to act ethically.*

CHAPTER 3

Why Leaders Fail to Act Ethically

ALTHOUGH SOCIETY HAS been intrigued about the behavior of leaders since the beginning of time, the actual formal study of leadership did not begin until the twentieth century. Some of the early academic research in this area was done by scholars such as Bernard Bass and Robert Stogdill, who studied leaders to determine if they possessed unique traits that made them successful. Throughout the twentieth century, leadership studies evolved, and scholars began to focus on the behavior of leaders. How did successful leaders interact with their followers? Consequently, various theories were developed such as transactional and transformational leadership, and the debate on whether leaders were born or made became more intensified. Most researchers began to conclude that while effective leaders may possess certain characteristics, leadership was a process that could be learned. Peter G. Northouse, a prominent leadership scholar, defined it in these terms: "Leadership is a process whereby an individual influences a group of individuals to achieve a common goal." A process connotes something that can be studied and learned. Thus, according to Northouse's definition, one can conclude that leaders can be made. Also implicit in this definition is the importance of the leader/follower relationship. Simply stated, without followers, there can be no leader. More importantly, the followers must be willing to trust and act in a manner consistent with the vision of the leader. In other words, effective leadership requires committed followership.

What makes people follow a leader? Is it the leader's charisma, ability to effectively communicate a vision, her intelligence, or her position? Although all of these may be important, I've concluded that the ability to influence is the most important asset in the leader's toolbox. Leadership, by definition, involves the ability to influence others. Consider some of the great leaders of the past and present. They all had or have an ability to influence the behavior of others. Dr. Martin Luther King influenced a nation of people to protest peacefully in the midst of violence being inflicted upon them. Hitler influenced a nation to adopt views of hatred and act out violently against those whom he saw as inferior and the primary impediment to accomplishing his goals. Osama bin Laden influenced his followers to sacrifice their lives and take the lives of innocent people to achieve his objectives. These three examples illustrate the importance of influence in the leader's ability to be effective. Without the ability to influence others to work toward a common goal, a leader will be ineffective. So where does the leader derive this ability to influence? The leader's ability to influence can be summed up in one word—*power*!

By virtue of having the title, every leader possesses a certain level of power. As stated in chapter 1, leaders possess one or more types of power. Based on the research of sociologists French and Raven, we know that leaders possess *personal* and *position* power. Position power is the result of the leader's status in the organization. For example, the chief operation officer (COO), due to her position, has what is known as reward and coercive power for those she exercise influence over. She has the ability to hire, promote, or grant bonuses as deemed necessary. In addition, she also has coercive power. That is the ability to use her powers to demote or reprimand to force her followers to carry out her wishes. These two types of position power, the ability to reward and coerce followers, give the leader the necessary tools she needs to influence behavior. When used properly, position power can be highly effective in enabling the leader to achieve the common goals of the group.

In addition to position power, leaders may also possess personal power. As stated earlier, the types of personal power that may be manifested by a leader are: expert, referent, and legitimate power. These types of power are considered by some to be the most important because they can exist independently of one's position. Let's look at an example of personal power and its ability to influence. One of the greatest tragedies in the twentieth century was the Jonestown Massacre, which occurred in 1978. On November 18, 1978, more than nine hundred people voluntarily followed the command of their leader Reverend Jim Jones and committed mass suicide. As a result of Jones's personal power, his followers literally "drank the Kool-Aid" and gave meaning to a phrase that has now grown to symbolize blind trust. Why did Jim Jones's followers make such a horrific decision? How was he able to influence his followers in such a manner? The answer is simple: he held a high degree of personal power over his followers. By most accounts, Jones was very charismatic and was an inspiring communicator. He was perceived by his followers as having a high level of expertise in biblical doctrine. Because of his expert and referent power, his followers were willing to be influenced even to their own detriment. The same may be said for the followers of Osama bin Laden and Adolf Hitler.

By now, you should recognize the important role power plays in the leader/follower relationship. As demonstrated in the previous examples, power can be used to achieve good results, but it can also be used to achieve evil results. If a leader uses power properly—that is, to achieve a good outcome—we may conclude that such power is used ethically. At this point, you may be thinking that an evil outcome may be perceived as good in the eyes of the leader or his followers. This is sometimes referred to as ethical or cultural relativity.

It is the "good is in the eye of the beholder" argument. For example, Hitler probably believed he was using his power to do good just as Martin Luther King most likely believed he was using his power to do good. In other words, both leaders subjectively believed they were using their power ethically. However, if their respective behavior was analyzed from a position of reason and objectivity, a rational, objective analysis would lead one to conclude that Hitler's use of power was ultimately unethical and that King's use of power was ethical. Therefore, when leaders fail to act ethically, it can generally be traced back to some misuse of power.

More times than not, unethical behavior can be traced to some level of misuse of *power* by those in leadership positions. Nowhere is this more evident than in the biblical figure King David. Dr. D. C. Ludwig and Dr. Clinton O. Longenecker wrote about David's breach of ethical behavior and appropriately described it as the Bathsheba syndrome. The story of David and Bathsheba is a fascinating story of lust and betrayal. David was a leader revered by his followers. He was said to be a man after God's own heart. As a leader, he possessed personal and position power. According to the scripture, David desired Bathsheba and ultimately had an affair with her. As a result of their affair, Bathsheba became pregnant. However, David's wrongful behavior did not stop there; he even sought to cover up his affair and ultimately engaged in behavior intended to result in the death of Bathsheba's husband. Was David conducting himself as an ethical leader? Evaluating his conduct from a position of reason and objectivity, one would inevitably conclude that David acted unethically. David's actions were not guided by concern for the well-being of others but solely by his own egocentric desire to have Bathsheba. David used his position of *power* to seduce her to be intimate with him and afterward attempted to use his *power* to cover up his unethical behavior. Did David know that his behavior was wrong? Do most leaders who engage in unethical behavior know that their behavior is wrong?

In his article addressing the ethical failures of leadership, Dr. Terry Price explores the volitional and cognitive aspect of leadership behavior. He asserts that leaders engage in wrongful behavior voluntarily, and more importantly, in most instances, they are fully aware that their behavior is wrong. King David knew that he was doing wrong. Governor Sanford knew that he was doing wrong. Bernie Madoff knew that he was doing wrong. Martha Stewart knew that she was doing wrong. If ethical failures of leadership are not based on a lack of understanding that the behavior is wrong, why do leaders behave unethically? Why do leaders misuse their power, often never showing concern for the interest of others?

The late comedian Flip Wilson in the early '70s popularized the phrase "The devil made me do it." By using this statement, he attempted to shift responsibility for his bad behavior to someone else. Could this be the reason leaders engage in unethical behavior? Implicit in this statement is the notion that wrongful behavior is not volitional but compelled by an outside force. While this assertion may explain the wrongful behavior of leaders from a theological perspective, many may find this reason to be simply an excuse for bad behavior. However, let's assume for argument's sake that a leader's actions are not volitional. For example, maybe he is under the influence of a drug. In fact, there is precedent for this line of thinking. In some criminal actions, the state of mind of a criminal defendant may serve as a mitigating factor when considering punishment. It does not excuse the behavior, but it can be considered in determining the level of punishment that should be assessed to the convicted person. So if a leader made certain decisions that were detrimental to his followers but the decision was made while under the influence or addiction to a controlled substance, one could argue that the leader's actions were not purely volitional. However, upon review of the ethical failings of most leaders, it appears that most bad behavior is voluntary with the leaders possessing complete knowledge of their wrongful actions. The essence of their ethical failure can be summed up in two words: *egoism* and *power*.

Prominent ethics scholar Joanne B. Ciulla asserts that ethics is at the heart of leadership. While I would agree with her statement, I believe egoism or egocentrism is at the heart of ethical *failures* of leadership. Simply stated, egoism is the ethical theory that self-interest is the proper motive for all human conduct. There are two forms of egoism that may be manifested in human behavior: ethical egoism and psychological egoism. Ethical egoism gained popularity through the work of the twentieth century philosopher Ann Rand, but many earlier philosophers such as Thomas Hobbes and David Hume wrote extensively about the value of pursuing one's own desires and pleasures. Ethical egoists believe that one has a moral duty to pursue one's own self-interest even if doing so means harming others. Another way of phrasing this theory is that no one's interest should take priority over your own interest. You have a moral duty to pursue the course of action that will bring you happiness. Many ethicists reject this theory for reasons I will discuss later.

Like ethical egoism, psychological egoism also supports pursing one's own interest; however, unlike ethical egoism, this theory does not consider pursuing one's self-interest to be a moral duty. Psychological egoism suggest that we all have a desire to pursue our self-interests; however, that desire can be abdicated as necessary in favor of the interest of others. This is exactly how most of us function. Let me give you a simple personal example to illustrate this point.

I'm an avid tennis fan and player. Over the past several months, I had been evaluating several tennis rackets with the expectation of making a purchase. My selfish interest was to spend a few hundred dollars to buy a new tennis racket. I really didn't need a new racket, but it was something I desired. Just about the time I was going to make my purchase, Haiti was hit by a massive, devastating earthquake. Although I desired to advance my own self-interest and purchase the rackets, I chose to abandon that desire and pursue a more altruistic approach and send the money to various charities to assist in the Haiti relief effort. Ethical egoism would dictate that I purchase the rackets—advance my own self-interest. Psychological egoism acknowledges that people have a tendency to pursue their self-interest first, but they often will abandon that interest to promote the interest of others. As you can see, psychological egoism can easily be reconciled with altruistic behavior.

Remember, one of the fundamental tenets of ethical behavior is showing concern for the interest of others. With that in mind, you should now be able to see the competing interests that exists between doing the right thing, which involves showing concern for the interest of others, and our innate tendency to want to advance our own interest. Ethics may require us to go against our natural desire to pursue the course of action that brings us the most benefit. If you consider the examples of unethical behavior that have been addressed thus far, and almost any other example you can imagine, you will quickly see the conflict between pursuing self-interests and showing concern for the interests of others. When both interests coincide, the course of action is simple. The men of Tuskegee wanted to be treated for their "bad blood," and the Department of Public Health doctors should have wanted to ensure that the men were cured of their "bad blood." Thus, when penicillin was discovered, there should not have been an ethical dilemma whether to stop the study. The decision must be to abandon the study and treat the men. Unfortunately, that was not what happened. Treatment was withheld to advance the self-interest of the public health scientists and physicians.

While egocentrism may be the reason for most unethical behavior, as previously stated, power is the fuel that facilitates that behavior. When leaders fail to act ethically, it generally can be traced to egocentrism *and* misuse of leadership power. Leaders engage in unethical behavior because they desire to advance their own self-interest and they possess the power to take the necessary actions to advance those interests. The challenge for the leader is to develop his ethical-reasoning skills to a level where he can assess ethical dilemmas reasonably, objectively and use his power appropriately to achieve the right results. In order to do this, leaders must rely heavily on two things: critical-thinking skills and discipline.

The ethical challenges many leaders face may not be as simple as the one faced by King David. A closer analysis of his dilemma would suggest that the resolution of ethical failures such as those on a personal level can be resolved through the application of self-discipline. The empirical evidence supports the notion that leaders misbehave fully cognizant of their wrongful actions and out of their own volition. Therefore, eliminating such behavior can be achieved by exercising proper self-control. By exercising proper discipline, Governor Mark Sanford could have avoided abandoning his position as governor of South Carolina while pursuing his personal desire to be with his mistress. While power may be the primary factor that facilitates unethical behavior, the lack of discipline or self-control is the factor that causes leaders to use their power to the detriment of others. Discipline alone, however, is not the solution. Leaders must develop critical-thinking skills that will enable them to analyze ethical dilemmas from a position of reason and objectivity. It is not enough to just make a decision because it feels like the right thing to do or a leader believes within his gut that it is the right thing to do.

CHAPTER 4

The Problem with Doing the Right Thing

DURING A RECENT television interview promoting her new book, a prominent financial analyst was asked to define integrity. She replied that integrity was simply "doing the right thing." As stated earlier, many people often define ethics as doing the right thing. Unfortunately, ethics and integrity are not as simple as just doing the right thing. In the eyes of the 9/11 terrorists, they were simply doing the right thing. Moreover, they carried out their mission with a high level of integrity. Hitler most likely believed he too was doing the right thing. The phrase has become a cliché term among many people to describe what it means to be ethical. In this chapter, I will explore in greater detail the inadequacy of reducing ethical behavior to such a simple notion. Moreover, I will probe into the implicit inference that doing the right thing is often obvious or innate and can occur without much reason or aforethought.

Are we born with the innate tendency to do the right thing? If one of the primary tenets of ethics is to show concern for the interest of others, are we naturally inclined to be unethical? These two questions go to the heart of the assertion that ethics is simply about doing the right thing. One could argue that we are naturally inclined to consider our own self-interest; it is a part of our basic survival instincts. Consider this fact: as children, we have an innate tendency to engage in psychological egoism. In early development, this tendency can be construed as a survival instinct. Children innately focus on themselves and their needs. Consequently, when they are hungry, they cry, regardless of the time of day or night. They don't consider whether Mom or Dad must get up and go to work the next morning; the focus is on their own self-interest. As children grow older and they develop the ability to communicate and reason, only then do they learn that sometimes it is necessary to abdicate their own self-interest in order to promote the interest of others.

We teach children the importance of sharing their toys or being courteous to others. Most adults would agree that sharing, being courteous, and just showing concern for the interest of others is the right thing to do, yet those are qualities that most often are taught. Doing the right thing is not something we instinctively do, especially when the right thing involves complex issues or situations that may place us in a compromising position. A few years ago, I asked my young daughter if she had taken her vitamins. Now she didn't particularly like the taste of the vitamins, thus her lack of enthusiasm about taking them. When I questioned her, she initially said, "Yes." However, I knew she could not have taken them because the seal on the bottle had not been broken. When I pressed her about it, she eventually told me that she had not taken the vitamins. Why did she resort to not telling me the truth? More importantly, where did she learn to be dishonest? Was she simply exercising her innate instinct to avoid a situation that she perceived to be unpleasant, being forced to chew those awfully tasting vitamins? Of course, as an adult, I can clearly see what the right course of behavior would have been.

Just like my daughter, sometimes leaders are faced with what on the surface may appear to be a simple ethical dilemma, yet they choose to engage in the wrong behavior. Unlike my daughter, they often know right from wrong and, notwithstanding that fact, choose to do the wrong thing. Doing the right thing is not something that we instinctively do. As illustrated through some of the examples given herein, it would appear that we often instinctively do the wrong thing. Doing the right thing requires leaders to adopt a process of reasoning and employing ethical strategies that will enable them to reason through complex ethical dilemmas. Can this behavior be taught?

Ethicists have debated the question of whether ethics can be taught for many years. Some conclude, such as Professor Thomas R. Piper and his colleagues in Harvard Business School's Program in Leadership, that it can be taught. During my lectures and training sessions, I often pose the same question to my students. Many often adamantly proclaim that you can't teach ethics. Some assert that ethics is something that either you have or you don't. In the preceding paragraphs, I attempted to demonstrate that being ethical is not something that is innate; therefore, one would think that it is something that we must be taught. I tend to believe not only that ethics can and should be taught but that it can and should be legislated as well. Now many people will argue that ethics cannot be legislated. I often present this question to my students, and usually, the majority concludes that ethics cannot be legislated. However, through further analysis, I usually can convince them that it can. While I will agree that moral behavior cannot be legislated, ethical behavior presents a different issue. Remember, one can draw a distinction between ethics and morality, the latter being personal values and the former being a manifestation of right and wrong behavior viewed from a societal perspective. This subtle distinction is what makes legislating ethical behavior possible. Let's look at a few examples to illustrate this point.

Corporations are made up of a diverse group of people. As a result, workers may have different or divergent views on what constitutes right or wrong behavior in the workplace. Some folks may feel that discrimination based on sexual orientation or gender is okay. It is a historical fact that for many years, gender and racial discrimination was practiced and considered an acceptable behavior in our culture. Today, many companies have codes of ethics that prohibit such behavior. These ethical codes consist of workplace rules designed to ensure that a certain level of behavior is practiced by everyone. Regardless of your moral beliefs, when working for a company that has a code of ethics, you are expected to display behavior consistent with the company's ethical standards. When I served in the military, our code of ethics prohibited discrimination based on gender or race. The ethical standard applied to all members of the armed forces, and anyone who violated that standard suffered consequences. As a result of establishing a code of behavior and mandating certain behavior that the military determined to be consistent with its culture, attitudes, over time, evolved. On July 26, 1948, President Truman signed Executive Order 9981, which ended segregation in the armed forces. This order ended the unethical practice of segregation. By mandating a change in behavior, this order paved the way for a change in attitudes. Today, the armed forces, while not totally free of all the vestiges of a segregated force, are a shining example of what equal opportunity can achieve. No longer are minorities and women precluded from reaching the pinnacle of military success. Nowhere is this more evident than in the rising of Colin Powell to the rank of general and chairman of the Joint Chiefs of Staff. When you change behavior, oftentimes you will change attitudes!

Another example of legislating ethical behavior can be seen through the implementation of some of our social laws. In 1964, Congress passed the Civil Rights Act (CRA), which prohibited certain types of discrimination. Prior to that passage of this act, women and minorities were routinely blatantly discriminated against in the workplace. It was not uncommon for African Americans or women to be denied employment or advancement solely because of their race or gender. By passing the Civil Rights Act, Congress was, in effect, legislating ethical behavior. The same can be said for the Americans with Disabilities Act, the Age Discrimination in Employment Act, and most recently, the Sarbanes-Oxley Act. All of these federal statutes seek to get people to simply "do the right thing." No one would be naive to think that such laws have eliminated all discriminatory behavior. However, when you evaluate the overall impact on society, one can reasonably conclude that the laws changed behavior, which gave impetus over time to changing attitudes. Thus, today we see far less unethical, disparate treatment and discrimination in the workplace. It is clear that by mandating a certain type of behavior, over time, societal attitudes changed.

Although legislating or mandating ethical behavior can result in ethical actions over time, making ethical decisions that result in the right outcomes also involves developing ethical-reasoning skills. Having good intentions or simply seeking to do the right thing is insufficient. Simply desiring to do good doesn't necessarily equate to a good or just outcome. When faced with a complex ethical dilemma, doing the right thing requires one to employ critical thinking and reasoning skills. A leader cannot just act based on his or her gut belief that he or she is doing the right thing. Sometimes, what appears to be the right thing may, in fact, be the wrong course of action when evaluated properly. The next chapter takes a look at the importance of ethical reasoning and ethics training in resolving complex ethical issues.

CHAPTER 5

Is Ethical Reasoning and Ethics Training Important?

ONE OF THE primary reasons that "doing the right thing" is an inadequate response when defining what it means to be ethical is, in part, because on the surface, it gives the impression that resolving complex ethical dilemmas is simple. More often than not, complex ethical dilemmas require one to engage in high-level ethical reasoning, incorporating critical-thinking skills that will facilitate choosing the right course of action based on reason and objectivity. Simply relying on one's gut feeling without a thorough analysis of the choices and impact of those choices may result in unethical behavior.

As stated in the previous chapter, being ethical is not innate. Moreover, instinctively doing what one believes to be right or exercising good intentions will not necessarily result in ethical behavior either. Only through a critical analysis of the facts and through developing ethical-reasoning skills can one reduce the chances of making unethical decisions. According to Professor Jerry Wind of the University of Pennsylvania's Wharton School of Business, "Business schools should really be teaching critical thinking more than anything else." The lack of critical-thinking skills in leaders was also called into question by Kepner-Tregoe's CEO Quinn Spitzer who said that the real issue facing leaders and organizations is the lack of critical-thinking skills in the workplace. He went on to state that the lack of critical-thinking skills in decision making can be seen readily in the business headlines. At the turn of the century, it was evident in the corporate scandals that plagued the business community such as Enron. In most recent times, it can be seen through the behavior of financial giants like Goldman Sachs and the many investment banks that engaged in the trading of consolidated debt obligations that ultimately caused the financial meltdown of 2008. Nora M. Braun, in her article titled "Critical Thinking in the Business Curriculum," states that the U.S. Department of Labor's Commission on Achieving Necessary Skills made the initial call to make critical-thinking skills a fundamental requirement for competing in today's global economy. There is a strong nexus between critical thinking and ethical decision making. More importantly, critical thinking is a learned behavior; therefore, it stands to reason that everyone has the ability to enhance their skills to make ethical decisions because everyone can become better critical thinkers.

Effective critical thinking involves several steps. They are as follows:

- Gather all pertinent information
- Analyze information to determine facts and reliable sources of evidence
- Assess relevance, truth, validity, and strength of information
- Recognize central thesis of arguments
- Address the logic of the arguments
- Identify cause-and-effect relationships

- Evaluate information from multiple perspectives and recognize one's own biases
- Draw conclusions and evaluate the effectiveness and justification of the conclusion
- Determine the criteria to use to evaluate options

Critical-thinking skills are very important when tackling complex ethical dilemmas. One of the most complex ethical decisions a president can make is whether to send a nation into war. Imagine if you were president of the United States and had to face the ethical dilemma of invading Iraq. It would be of critical importance to ensure that you gather all pertinent facts and to assess the reliability of the sources of the information. In retrospect, it appears that much of the information that was relied upon in making the decision to invade Iraq was unreliable or very biased. The argument for invading shifted from WMDs (Weapons of Mass Destruction) to regime removal, and it appears that decision makers did not fully reflect on the cause and effect. In other words, how would removing Iraq's leader impact Iran and the Middle East's stability? What about the logic of our invasion argument? Is the doctrine of preemption a rational policy?

If the doctrine of preemption were applied by every nation, would we not be in a perpetual state of war? What if bickering neighbors applied the doctrine of preemption? Fortunately, under our system of jurisprudence, a self-defense argument cannot be raised based on the capability of someone to do harm to another. Applying the critical-thinking steps outlined above would lead one to conclude that reasonable minds could come to a different decision regarding whether the invasion of Iraq was the proper thing to do. Although history will be the judge of that decision, one thing is certain, and that is, resolving complex ethical issues must include critical thinking.

Operating from the premise that critical thinking is a key component of ethical reasoning and further assuming that those skills can be taught, one might naturally conclude that ethics training should be incorporated into the culture of every organization that is concerned about ethical decision-making. Is ethics training relevant? What is its impact on corporate behavior? Among the many priorities organizational leaders face, ensuring long-term survivability must be of paramount concern. Engaging in activities that will avoid corporate liability is tantamount to achieving longevity within the business arena. Dating back to the mid 1950s, corporate America has experienced a widening gap in society's expectations of ethical business behavior and the actual ethical conduct of business organizations. Since the turn of the century and well into the twenty-first century, many organizations and leaders within those organizations have faced civil and criminal charges as a result of conduct that was unethical or illegal. Could formal ethics training affect the liability these organizations may face as a result of the unethical conduct of their employees? Is ethics training needed in today's workplace?

Unethical behavior in the workplace should be of critical importance to every leader or manager in today's organizations. It impacts both human resources and the economic performance of organizations. From a human resources perspective, employees value and expect ethical behavior within their organizations. A study by the Ethics Resource Center indicated that 90 percent of workers believe that their companies should do "what is right, not just what is profitable." Notwithstanding the desire to do what is right, the Ethics Officer Association found that 48 percent of managers and executives reported having been involved in an illegal or unethical issue in the past year, and 57 percent reported that they found the pressure to be unethical getting worse over time. Criminal and unethical workplace behavior causes losses for U.S. industry of approximately $400 billion per year. In addition, employee malfeasance in areas such as discrimination, safety procedures, and trade practices results in expensive judgments against organizations. In the best of all possible worlds, the conscience of each individual employee would be sufficient to maintain ethical workplace practices. However, an individual's values and moral code may be ignored as a result of the pressures and difficult choices faced in daily decision-making. In addition, employees' potential unethical behavior has repercussions for others in the organization and for the organization itself. Ethical decision-making and behavior are, therefore, the responsibility and challenge of both the individual and the organization. Within the organization, it is the responsibility of managers and leaders to determine the most effective means of disseminating information and creating expectations about ethical behavior.

By establishing strong ethics programs and conducting effective ethics training, leaders can avoid civil and criminal liability, which will negatively impact the organization. Ethics training is important not only to promote an ethical environment and culture but to serve as a defense from liability. U.S. courts have long recognized the doctrine of respondeat superior as a legal basis for holding organizations vicariously liable for the conduct of their employees. This doctrine serves as the basis for holding companies liable for unethical behavior that may result in sexual harassment and other forms of unethical conduct such as racial discrimination. Employees who engage in unethical behavior literally cost organizations millions of dollars. For example, the unethical conduct of sexual harassment and racial discrimination has resulted in large corporations like Mitsubishi Motor Manufacturing of America, Ford Motor Company, and Coca-Cola to settle lawsuits in excess of $230 million. What can organizations do to avoid such liability? In 1998, the United States Supreme Court, through its rulings in *Burlington v. Ellerth* and *Faragher v. Boca Raton*, clearly articulated that training could serve as a defense to civil liability. If a company has a policy addressing the unethical behavior of sexual harassment and provides training to ensure that employees understand that such behavior is unacceptable in the workplace, that organization will have an effective defense from civil liability.

Although ethics training may avoid corporate liability, that is not the only reason organizations should invest in formal ethics training. Empirical research suggests that the right type of ethics training can have a positive effect on the behavior of employees. In addition, it can help set the ethical climate of the organization. According to an article by Delaney and Sockell in the *Journal of Business Ethics*, ethical training positively impacts the employee's feelings toward ethical behavior. Moreover, they found that employees in organizations with ethics training programs are more likely to have refused to engage in unethical behavior. Another study by Loe and Weeks published in the *Journal of Personal Selling and Sales Management* suggests that the use of role plays and contingency-based scenario training may improve the ethical reasoning of sales people. Finally, according to a study conducted by B. Stevens and published in the *Journal of Business Ethics*, employees report training as the best venue for learning about organizational and expectations for ethical behavior. Although the evidence is conclusive that ethics training can have a positive impact on employees' attitudes and behavior, the method of training is critical to achieving the desired outcome. What type of ethics training is most effective?

Ethics training is often conducted using videotapes, lectures, role play, or games. However, a recent large study on this topic sheds some insight on what type of training is most effective. Based on a survey of ten thousand randomly selected employees of six U.S. companies, Trevino, Weaver, Gibson, and Toffler, in their article "Managing Ethics and Legal Compliance: What Works and What Hurts," found that the least effective ethics training is the canned product delivered by an outside consultant. The most effective training design, shown to be related to reduced observation of unethical behavior, is one in which each manager is responsible for training his or her direct reports and engaging these employees in discussions regarding job-specific ethical dilemmas. Although direct management involvement increases the effectiveness of ethics training programs, there are some essential features of a formal ethics training program that can ensure effectiveness as well. Ponemon and Felo, in their study analyzing the essential features of effective ethics training program, came up with the following:

- Live instruction
- Small class size
- Significant group interaction
- A minimum of four hours of instruction
- Separation of ethical consideration and legal-requirements issues
- Follow-up communications such as ethics newsletters and informal ethics workgroups

Although ethics training will not ensure that employees will always behave in an ethical manner, it increases *awareness* and promotes a proper *ethical climate* within the organization. By providing ethics training, employees are able to see a commitment from senior leaders to invest the time and money in an effort to build and promote an ethical organization. Through ethics training, employees are exposed to moral reasoning and are taught the principles of utilitarianism and the categorical imperative of duty-based ethics as a framework for making decisions. Consequently, when employees have the opportunity to apply these principles in training, they are able to draw on the training experience in similar real-world situations.

CHAPTER 6

Ethicality of Transactional versus Transformational Leadership

WHEN LEADERS FAIL to do the right thing, the courts, legislature, and administrative agencies are forced to intervene and either make a wrong right or implement laws to preclude future breaches of ethical behavior. According to Laura Nash in her best-selling book entitled *Good Intentions Aside: A Manager's Guide to Resolving Ethical Problems*, most leaders have good intentions, and unethical behavior is often the result of moral rationalization. However, despite good intentions, corporate leaders have a tendency to deny those activities and decisions that would be damaging to their self-image if examined dispassionately. Leaders have a tendency to judge their intentions as "good" even when the facts state otherwise.

Assuming that unethical behavior is often the result of good intentions, what can leadership do to ensure that good intentions lead to good behavior? In order to ensure that good intentions lead to good behavior, the organization must first have good, ethical leadership. Leadership that is capable of (1) identifying ethical issues when they inevitably arise, (2) leadership that utilizes an ethical decision-making process for resolving ethical disputes, and (3) leadership that has the courage to make the ethical decision. Although many theories and styles of leadership exist, is there a style of leadership more conducive for resolving ethical issues?

Two very popular leadership styles are transformational and transactional leadership. During corporate training sessions, I often ask participants what they would rather be, transformational or transactional; and most respond by saying transformational. I suspect this is, in part, because transformational leaders are perceived as being more ethical than transactional leaders. However, is this really the case? Well, before exploring that question, let's look at the fundamental difference between transactional and transformational leadership.

James McGregor Burns introduced the term *transformational leadership* in 1978. Much of the scholarly work on this subject has been based on Burns's ideas. He described transformational leadership as an interaction between leaders and followers, which raises the individuals to higher levels of motivation and morality. Self-interests are transcended for the greater good. Dr. Bernard Bass expounded on this theory of leadership by proposing a model of transformational and transactional leadership. In his model, Bass defined transactional leadership as leadership that emphasizes transactional exchanges that takes place among leaders, colleagues, and followers. Based on the definition, one might presume that one style is better than the other. Although the empirical research does not make this claim, it does appear that most leaders tend to be transactional. However, by focusing specifically on the transactional exchanges between the leader and follower to achieve results, the door inevitably is open for unethical behavior. For example, a leader of a sales team using transactional exchanges to achieve results. The leader tells his follower that "if you sell so many widgets, you will receive a large bonus." The follower is now motivated by the desire to receive the bonus. As pressure mounts to make the sale, the focus will most likely be on the transactional exchange—sales equals bonus—rather than on being concerned whether the sales are done in an ethical manner. Now that is not to say that the follower will always behave in an amoral manner, but the emphasis in a transactional exchange is less likely to be on the ethicality of the exchange. Again, according to Burns, transactional leadership essentially involves an exchange between leader and subordinate such that each receives something from the other in return for something else. In this situation, the focus is primarily on the transactional exchange. Therefore, can one make the assumption that transactional leadership is devoid of ethical behavior?

The notion that transactional leadership often leads to unethical behavior is based on the assertion that transactional leadership is primarily focused on the bottom line. In a for-profit environment, the bottom line is often the generation of profits. Nowhere is this more evident than in the recent Wall Street crisis, which resulted in a financial meltdown. Many of the financial institutions were focused so much on the bottom line of making profits that they assumed unreasonable risks in buying and selling instruments that they subsequently found out were basically worthless. The late free market economist Milton Friedman, in his popular *New York Times* article "The Social Responsibility of Business Is to Increase Its Profits," acknowledged that such behavior must be engaged consistently with law and widely shared ethical customs. Moreover, Bass stated that ethics of leadership, whether transformational or transactional, rests on three pillars: (1) the moral character of the leader; (2) the values of the leader's vision, articulation, and program, which followers choose whether or not to embrace; and (3) the morality of the processes and actions that the leaders engage in and pursue. By incorporating these pillars into their leadership style, even a transactional leader will be less likely to abdicate his ethical responsibility in an effort to achieve the bottom line. The third pillar is very important because even an ethical outcome may be tarnished if an unethical process is used to achieve it. The case of *Loomis v. Gardner*, which will be addressed in greater detail later, illustrates the importance of leaders using an ethical process to achieve a desired result.

The relationship between employers and employees is replete with ethical challenges. One situation that often raises ethical concerns is the termination of an employee. Due process requirements may establish a legal cause of action when an employee is terminated without following proper procedures. By definition, due process simply means the process that a person is due to ensure fairness. Typically, that means the individual is entitled to notice and an opportunity to rebut the allegations. However, compliance with the legal requirements may still raise ethical questions on whether the employer did the right thing. Notwithstanding the employment-at-will doctrine, which allows an employer to terminate an employee for any reason or no reason, absent a contract, many federal and state statutes protect employees from termination at the whim of their employers. Courts and legislators recognized the inequality of bargaining power between employer and employee and that the inability of employees to protect themselves from unjust and oftentimes unethical actions by their employers has not just economic ramifications but also emotional and social ramifications. One of the primary reasons that the employment relationship often raises ethical concerns is because for most individuals, the terms of the employment contract are imposed on a "take it or leave it" basis by the corporate employer. The employee lacks the equal bargaining power to protect himself. Studies also show that the dependence on the employment relationship is not just economic. Within the employment relationship, the employee seeks fulfillment of many of his needs for social status and identity. Therefore, the employment relationship is one that requires fairness when discharge is being considered. In order to ensure this fairness, several exceptions to the employment-at-will doctrine have been established.

Many of the limitations on the ability of the employer to discharge employees at will arise from tort and contract law. The most significant limitation on the employment-at-will doctrine deriving from tort law is a cause of action for wrongful discharge based on public policy claims. These claims are consistent with ethical principles of justice and fairness and formed the legal basis for Kevin Gardner in his lawsuit against Loomis Armored Inc.

Gardner was an armored-car guard and driver for the Loomis Armored Company. Loomis's policy required that at least one of the guard/drivers remain in the armored car at all times. Loomis's employee handbook made it clear that the penalty for violating the rule was termination of employment. The purpose of this rule was to ensure the safety of the driver and the guard who delivered the money into the business premises. During one of the regular customer stops, at a bank branch, Gardner, who had remained in the armored car consistent with company policy, observed the bank branch manager, whom he knew from previous deliveries, running from the building and being chased by a man wielding a knife. The bank manager ran in front of Gardner's armored car and screamed for help. Gardner looked around and, seeing no one coming to assist her, got out of the armored car, locking the door behind him. He then chased the knife-wielding man back into the bank, where the man was tackled to the floor and disarmed. The Loomis Armored Company subsequently fired Gardner for violating the company rule. Gardner filed a wrongful discharge claim, arguing that the termination violated public policy, alleging that one should not be fired for violating a company rule when the motivation was attempting to assist another who was in danger of serious physical injury or death. Historically, the public policy exception to the employee-at-will doctrine was narrowly construed to apply to only specific types of claims and to those claims protected by a state or federal statute. Fortunately for Gardner, the Washington Supreme Court was persuaded by his final argument that a "fundamental public policy . . . clearly evidenced by countless statutes and judicial decisions" that places the highest priority on human life and that encourages people to go to each other's assistance does exist. Although Gardner did not cite any specific state or federal statute expressly requiring one to go to another's assistance, the Washington Supreme Court adopted a more liberal and expansive interpretation of the public policy exception in supporting Gardner's wrongful-discharge claim.

As a result of the Washington Supreme Court's ruling, Loomis's termination of Gardner was held to be illegal. Loomis's conduct resulted in litigation cost and possibly negative publicity for the organization. However, aside from the legal implications, the larger ethical question is, did Loomis do the right thing? The Washington Supreme Court seems to suggest that the "right thing" was to value the preservation of human life over the rigid interpretation of a corporate policy. Was the Loomis leadership being transformational or transactional?

Unlike transactional leadership, the transformational leader places a higher emphasis on the moral development of the follower. Since first articulated by James MacGregor Burns in 1978, transformational leadership has become one of the most dominant paradigms of leadership studies. Transformational leadership is a construct of leadership that focuses on the moral development of the followers. Although not without scholarly criticism, research suggests that transformational leadership creates an organizational climate that is more conducive to ethical behavior than transactional leadership. Transformational leadership involves four components: (1) individual consideration of each follower's needs; (2) intellectual stimulation of followers, focusing on their unique strengths; (3) inspirational motivation of followers to be their best self; and (4) idealized influence to align the interest and vision of the followers with those of the organization and develop followers to their fullest potential.

Transformational leaders inspire their followers to share in the mutually rewarding visions of success while enabling and empowering them to convert the visions into reality. Because the transformational leader is concerned not just with the bottom line but also with the development of the employee, his actions are guided by a concomitant concern for the employee and the organization. The transformational leader works sincerely with followers to determine and achieve the mutual interests of both. A transformational leader makes decisions with the interest of the follower stakeholder paramount. He places less emphasis on contingent rewards, which could lead to moral rationalization for purposes of achieving the bottom line. The transformational leader, through idealized influence and inspirational motivation, seeks to be a positive role model and mentor. His focus is not just to align the follower's interest with those of the organization but to ensure the moral development of the follower. A true transformational leader would avoid making self-centered decisions but decisions with the mutual benefit of the organization and follower in mind. This type of leadership stresses human development, relationships of reciprocal trust, and the resolution of values/conflicts to the mutual satisfaction of the respective parties.

When leaders are truly transformational and serve as role models of ethical behavior, a positive culture will permeate the whole organization. However, it is important to understand that not all leaders who espouse to be transformational leaders are indeed transformational ones. Some leaders are what Bernard M. Bass refers to as pseudotransformational leaders. Bass refers to true transformational leaders as people like Mahatma Gandhi and Martin Luther King Jr. Pseudotransformational leadership may appear to be transformational, but the real objective of the leader is about maintaining the dependence of their followers. They may create the impression that they are doing the right thing but secretly fail to do so when doing the right thing conflicts with their own narcissistic interests. However, the true transformational leader is concerned about the development of followers into ethical leaders. True transformational leaders openly bring about changes in the followers' values by the merit and relevancy of the leaders' ideas and mission to their followers' ultimate benefit and satisfaction. Therefore, in the case of *Loomis v. Gardner,* a transformational leader would have found a way to reconcile the company's rule of never leaving the vehicle with the heroic behavior of the follower versus firing him.

Both transactional and transformational leaders will face ethical dilemmas. However, the transactional leader must place greater concern to ensure that the focus on the bottom line does not compromise the importance of engaging in ethical behavior.

CHAPTER 7

Strategies for Resolving Ethical Dilemmas

ETHICS TRANSCENDS EVERYTHING we do. Think about it; most, if not all, decisions made by today's leaders may have an ethical component. Consequently, a leader may choose to be amoral, which means he does not consider the ethical consequences of the component of his decision. An amoral leader functions as though ethics does not exist. A leader may also choose to be immoral and ignore the ethical ramifications of his actions. This leader consciously chooses to engage in the behavior with complete knowledge that his behavior is wrong (e.g.,

King David's actions with Bathsheba). Finally, a leader may choose to be moral and consider the ethical impact of his decision. Of course, the latter is the desired course of action. Ideally, all decisions should be made taking into consideration the ethical ramifications of one's actions. Whether a leader is deciding to lay off an employee or promote an employee, the ethicality of the leader's action must be considered. In this chapter, I will put forth several strategies that will facilitate ethical decision making. I call these the *seven strategies for resolving ethical dilemmas.*

Is It Legal?

When considering the ethicality of an action, the first thing the leader must do is consider whether the action is legal. As previously stated, one of the paramount concerns of a leader must be the long-term survival of the organization. Corporations are legal entities that can be sued and charged with crimes. When a leader engages in behavior that is illegal, it opens up the organization for civil liability and, possibly, criminal prosecution. Such actions can result in large fines and negative publicity, which may result in declining sales and market share and may ultimately lead to bankruptcy of the organization as what occurred with Enron. Determining whether an action is legal or not is pretty simple. There are people trained to provide assistance in this area. They are called lawyers. In the United States, all crimes are codified, so there is no excuse for a leader unknowingly engaging in criminal behavior. If there is an area of doubt, that so-called gray area, you should err on the side of caution and not run the risk of violating the law, regardless of the benefits. Although ethical behavior is not required, legal behavior is so never straddle the line. Always follow the law, it is your duty to your organization.

Does It Harm Others?

Although complying with the law is required, being ethical is not; it is a desired outcome. Therefore, when faced with an ethical dilemma and based on the ethical principles addressed in this book, one of the first factors that must be taken into consideration is whether the decision will cause harm to others. By incorporating this fundamental principle of ethics, showing concern for the interest of others, you may avoid making an unethical decision. However, it is important to make something perfectly clear; the ethical course of action does not necessarily mean that you will never cause harm. Sometimes, the ethical course of action may result in others being harmed. For example, eminent domain results in harming the minority for the greater societal good. The focus here is to minimize harm to others. The leader should always strive to seek the course of action that minimizes harm while producing an ethical result. A decision to rightsize will inevitably harm the person being laid off. However, giving that person sufficient notice, providing them with severance if possible, and providing alternative-job training are all things that can mitigate the harm. The simple fact of showing concern for the interest of others may result in a decision being modified because upon analysis, the leader may discover that the perceived benefit does not outweigh the harm that will ensue.

Does It Pass the CNN Test?

I had a former boss tell me that "visibility is good, but exposure will kill you." He was encouraging me to take the jobs that will bring visibility to my strengths and avoid jobs that will expose my weaknesses. There is also an old saying that transparency is the best disinfectant. Well, the same applies when it comes to our actions. When resolving an ethical dilemma, a leader should consider how he would feel if his actions were publicized to the entire world on CNN. Would you be comfortable with your decision if it was the main topic of discussion on *Anderson 360* and you knew you were being subjected to public disclosure and critique? I think if the former CEO and CFO of Enron had considered that their actions were going to be subjected to public disclosure, they probably would have chosen a different course of action. If the former CEO had known that it would have been publicly disclosed that he was dumping shares of Enron stock while encouraging others to buy, he probably would not have made that unethical decision.

Get a Second Opinion

In the field of healthcare, it is a common practice to seek second and sometimes third opinions. Although your primary physician may be a board-certified expert in his chosen field, seeking a second opinion is a form of validation. It also may provide other options that may not have been on the table. The same applies to resolving ethical dilemmas. A leader would be well served to seek the advice of a trusted advisor, who he feels will give him an unbiased, objective opinion. That person may be an expert in the field, who can point out factors you may not have considered, or it may be someone whom you believe to have a good moral compass. Let me caution you here that getting a second opinion does not mean that you abdicate your responsibility because ultimately, as the leader, the buck stops with you. It is your decision, and you must bear the responsibility. However, the second opinion may reveal some factors that you may have not considered. In addition, if the person has a good moral compass, their confirmation can be reassuring that you are going down the right road.

Does It Pass the Ambien Test?

Ambien is a prescription sleep aid used for the treatment of insomnia. Insomnia is a sleep disorder characterized by difficulty falling and/or staying asleep. Now I'm sure you never thought insomnia to be an ethical condition; however, if your decision agonizes you and causes you to stay awake at night, you have probably not made the right decision. By the same token, if you can lie down and go to sleep after making your decision without the need for Ambien, you may have made the proper decision. Assuming that you are not a psycho or sociopath, you should be troubled when you make a decision that is blatantly unethical. The physicians and scientists participating in the Tuskegee study should have been troubled that once penicillin was available, they refused to treat the subjects of the study. They should have had difficulty sleeping at night. They should have needed Ambien to fall asleep! Now, assuming that they made the right decision, there should be no agonizing over it and the need for Ambien for *that* decision should not exist—test passed!

Does It Pass the Socrates Test?

Socrates is the ancient Greek philosopher who is given credit for setting the agenda for the tradition of critical thinking. I can recall my first year of law school and being exposed to the Socratic method of teaching, which is specifically designed to enhance critical-thinking skills. When faced with an ethical dilemma, a leader must ensure that the resolution is not reached based solely on gut feelings or the subjective desire to do the right thing. Yes, good intentions are important. Doing the right thing is important, but the process of getting to the right result must be based on reason and objectivity. Therefore, employing the principles of critical thinking outlined in chapter 6 will enhance the likelihood that the leader will reach a just and ethical outcome.

Does It Make God Smile?

At the end of the day, the final question the leader should consider is, does the chosen course of action make God or the higher power of your choosing smile? I use God loosely here, and I'm not advocating any particular religion or faith. For those who may be atheist or agnostic, you may substitute God for your mother or any other figure you revere. I also must point out that I'm speaking of an unconditionally loving God, who is concerned with only good, not the God depicted in the Old Testament of the Bible or the God who condones torturing souls in eternal damnation. The point here is simply to look to a source beyond you that you feel reflect the characteristics of good and of being one's best self. In legal parlance, we use the term the *prudent* or *reasonable person standard*. This is the person who goes through life exercising proper judgment and engaging in the right course of action under the circumstances. It is an objective standard that can be used as a benchmark for how one should act under certain situations. So if God would look at your decision and smile at your actions, you've probably done the right thing!

CHAPTER 8

Conclusion

MANY OF THE challenges faced by organizations can be attributed to a lack of leadership. Why do I make this assertion you might ask? Well, it is rather simple. Leaders are ultimately responsible for developing vision and allocating resources to achieve predetermined objectives. When those objectives are not met, the leader has not been effective. The role of being an effective leader inevitably involves making decisions. Many of those decisions have ethical dimensions that must be resolved in an ethical manner. Resolving dilemmas ethically is often equated with doing the right thing. While on the surface this may be true, desiring to do the right thing is not enough. As addressed in the preceding paragraphs, ethical decision making involves a process and an understanding of what it means to be ethical. Desiring to do the right thing is a great start, but it must be complemented with an equal desire to learn how to employ ethical-reasoning skills to ensure that what appears to be the right thing is in fact the *right* thing.

This book has provided a working definition of ethics, specifically addressing the subtle distinction between ethics and morality. Understanding this distinction is important because while both address the conduct of right and wrong, the subjective nature of moral behavior can lead to conflict when applied from a societal perspective. Ethics seeks to establish a standard of behavior that all can comply with, regardless of their personal mores. In today's global environment, the workplace consists of diverse groups. Gender, ethnicity, sexual orientation, age, and diversity of thought all serve to create a workforce in which varying views can result in different perspectives of right and wrong. Therefore, in order to ensure that all employees have a common understanding of what behavior is considered acceptable and, more importantly, what behavior is considered unacceptable, organizations often establish a formal code of ethics. A code of ethics seeks to formalize or codify a universal standard of behavior for all members of that organization. Although having such a code is a good thing, no code of ethics can cover every situation. Therefore, it is important that leaders ensure that they set the ethical climate for their organizations and, more importantly, equip their followers with the tools to engage in ethical reasoning. It is important that we teach ethics and, in some cases, legislate ethics.

The first step in teaching ethics is to define ethics properly. The simplistic definition associated with ethics—doing the right thing—must be qualified. Yes, ethics is about doing the right thing, but it also involves so much more. Ethics is about doing the right thing when the right thing is evaluated from a position of reason and objectivity. Moreover, it is important to understand that ethical behavior may not always be consistent with the disciplines of law or religion. Sometimes, what is legal may not be ethical. For years, eugenics laws were legal in some states, which resulted in the state having the right to sterilize women under certain circumstances. A reasoned ethical view would find such a law troubling. So while law and religion clearly have a role in ethical decision-making, it is important to recognize that ethical reasoning must also be independent of those disciplines.

Once ethics has been adequately defined, it is necessary to understand the primary reasons people fail to behave ethically. Pursuing ones self-interest, notwithstanding its impact on others, will often lead to unethical decision-making. As stated earlier, we all have a tendency to engage in egoism, but ethics demands that when necessary, we abdicate our selfish interest when it will cause harm to others. Behind every unethical decision, you will usually find some level of egocentrism. Recently, there has been what appears to be a high level of marital infidelity involving public figures. Now this may be attributed to our seemingly insatiable appetite for infotainment or to the expanded media coverage into private affairs, but regardless of the reason, behind each act of infidelity is a party pursing his or her own self-interest without showing regard for the interest of others. It would appear that the individuals involved in these actions failed to engage in ethical reasoning, which demands that one shows regard for the interest of others.

Ethical reasoning is critically important to effective ethical decision-making. A desire to make ethical decisions or a desire to do the right thing is not enough. One must be equipped with the necessary tools to resolve complex ethical dilemmas and not simply rely on one's *good intentions* to just do the right thing. In this book, I've outlined seven strategies that will facilitate ethical reasoning and decision making. When faced with an ethical dilemma, following these strategies will give you a framework to make the best decision that will ensure you to do not only the right thing but the ethical thing!

CPSIA information can be obtained at www.ICGtesting.com
Printed in the USA
LVOW120939040112

262333LV00002B/14/P